Leaping Learners
Education, LLC

For more information and resources visit us at:

www.leapinglearnersed.com

Photo Credits

Monkey graphic © dreamblack46/stock.adobe.com

Cover, © robynmac/stock.adobe.com; Pg. 1-2 © max_776/stock.adobe.com; Pg. 5-6 © salparadis/stock.adobe.com; Pg. 9-10 © mtilghma/stock.adobe.com; Pg. 20 © skynet/stock. adobe.com, © bodnarinq/stock.adobe.com

All design by Sean Bulger
All other pictures by Sean Bulger or royalty free from Pixabay.com

ISBN
978-1-948569-13-2

Dear Parents and Guardians,

Thank you for purchasing a *Matt Learns About* series book! After teaching students from kindergarten to second grade for more than seven years, I became frustrated by the lack of engaging books my students could read independently. To help my students engage with nonfiction topics, my wife and I decided to write nonfiction books for children. We hope to inspire young children to learn about the natural world.

Here at Leaping Learners Education, LLC, we have three main goals:

1. Spark young readers' curiosity about the natural world
2. Develop critical independent reading skills at an early age
3. Develop reading comprehension skills before and after reading

We hope your child enjoys learning with Matt. If you or your children are interested in a topic we have not written about yet, send us an email with your topic, and maybe your book will be next!

Thank you,

Sean Bulger, Ed.M

www.leapinglearnersed.com

Reading Suggestions:

Before reading this book, encourage your children to do a "picture walk," where they skim through the book and look at the pictures to help them think about what they already know about the topic. Thinking about what they already know helps children get excited about learning more facts and begin reading with some confidence.

Preview any new vocabulary words with your child. Key vocabulary words are found on the last few pages of the book. Have your children use the new phrases in their own words to see if they understand the definition.

After previewing the book, encourage your children to read the book independently more than once. After they have read it, ask them specific questions related to the information in the book. Encourage them to go back and reread the relevant section in the book to retrieve the answer in case they forgot the facts.

Finally, see if your child can complete the reading comprehension exercises at the end of the book to strengthen their understanding of the topic!

This book is best for ages 6-8
but. . .
Please be mindful that reading levels are a guide and vary depending on a child's skills and needs.

Matt Learns About . . . Rainforests

Written by Sean and Anicia Bulger

Table of Contents

Hi! My name is Matt. I love to discover and learn new things. In this book, we will learn about rainforests. Let's go!

Introduction

Rainforests are hot, tropical forests around the world that are home to many plants and animals.

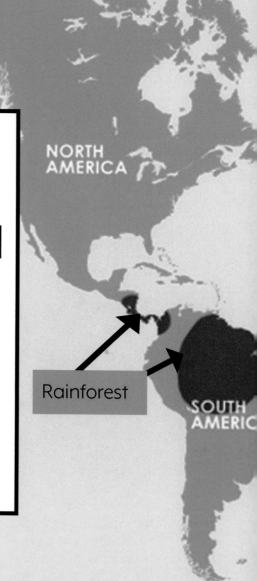

NORTH AMERICA

Rainforest

SOUTH AMERIC

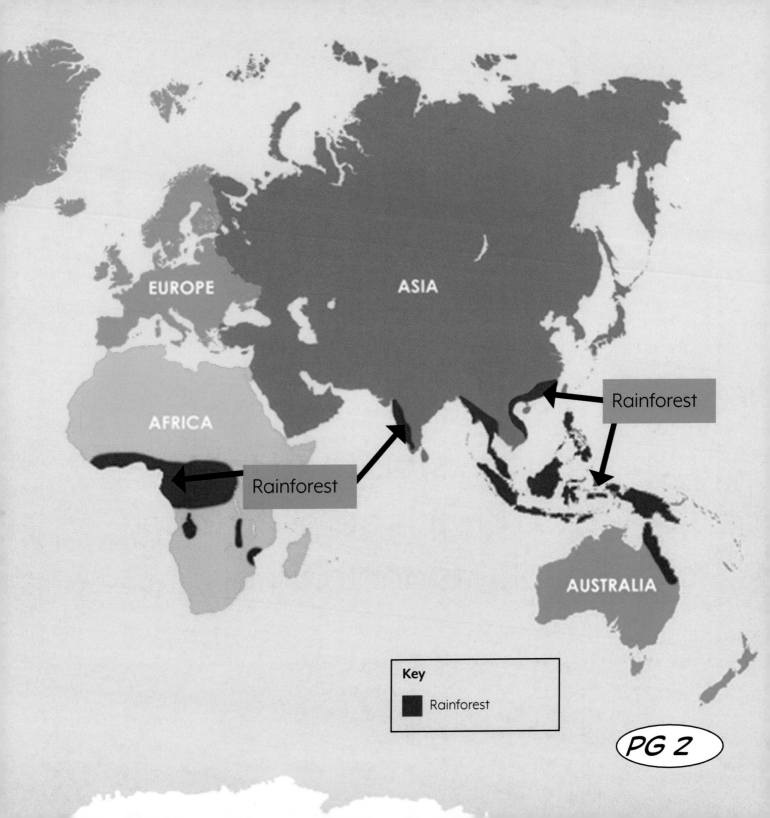

Key

Rainforest

What do rainforests look like?

Tricky Words:
say
E-merg-ent
can-o-pee

Rainforests have four layers. These layers are called the emergent, canopy, understory, and the forest floor. Each layer is home to many different plants and animals.

Emergent

Canopy

Understory

Forest Floor

PG 4

Emergent Layer

The emergent layer is the highest layer of the rainforest. This layer gets a lot of sunlight. It is very hot.

PG 6

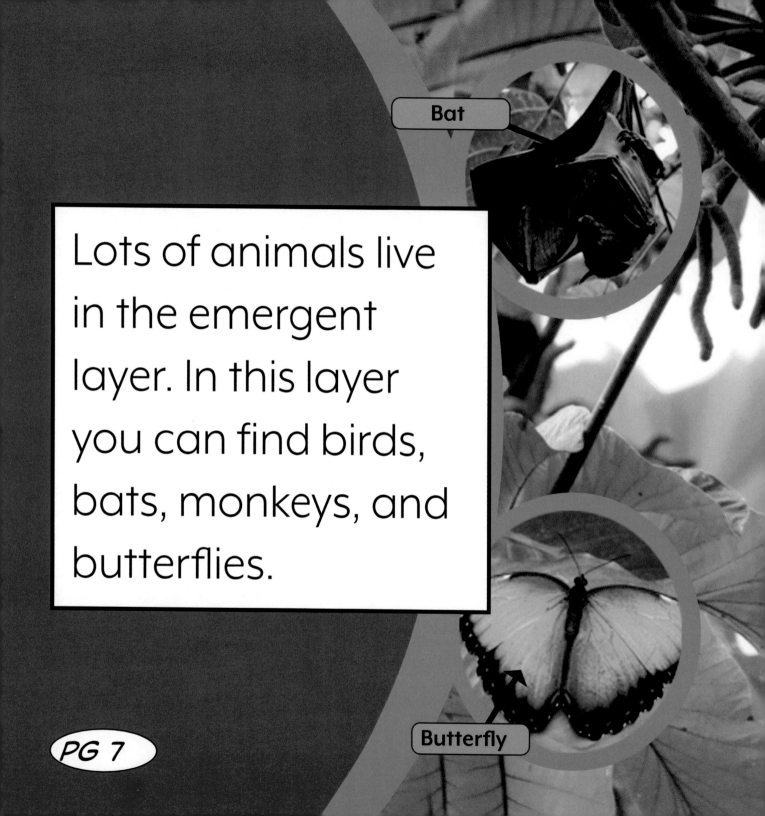

Lots of animals live in the emergent layer. In this layer you can find birds, bats, monkeys, and butterflies.

Bat

Butterfly

Canopy

The canopy layer is below the emergent layer. It gets less sunlight than the emergent layer. There are lots of leaves and **vines** growing here.

PG 10

The canopy layer is home to the most animals. It has lots of food for animals to eat. Some animals that live here are sloths and monkeys.

Which animals live in the canopy?

Sloth

Animals that live in the canopy get around by hopping, flying, climbing, and jumping. They **communicate** to each other using special calls and noises.

Tricky word:
Say

co-mun-i-cate

Monkey

Understory

The understory is below the canopy. It does not get a lot of sunlight. Plants in this layer need to have big leaves to get sunlight.

PG 14

Frog

The understory is home to many **dangerous** animals. Some animals that live there are jaguars and **poisonous** frogs.

Tricky words: chunk them out
dan-ger-ous
poi-son-ous

Jaguar

Forest Floor

The forest floor is the lowest layer. It gets almost no sunlight or wind. Not many plants grow on the forest floor since there is not much sunlight.

PG 18

Anteater

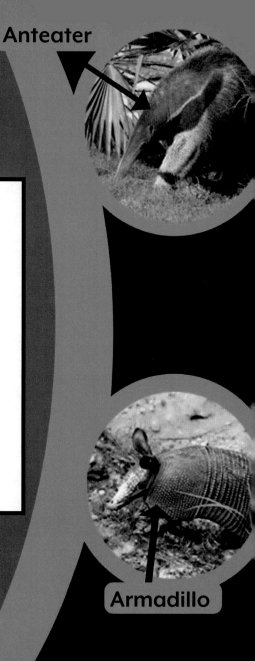

Some animals that live on the forest floor are ants, giant anteaters, and armadillos.

Armadillo

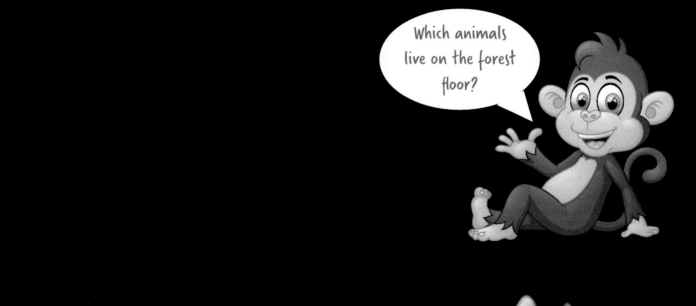

Ant

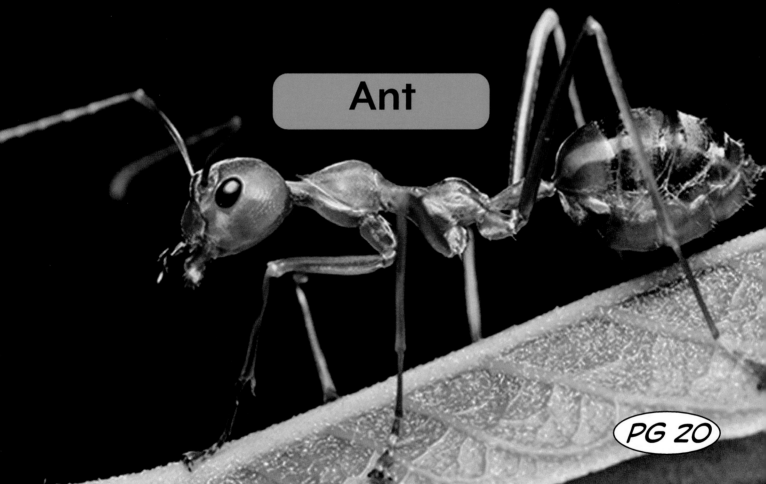

Rainforest Plants

Rainforests have many different plants. Plants live in all the layers, but most live in the emergent and canopy layers.

What are plants in the rainforest like?

Rainforest plants can be all different colors, shapes, and sizes. Plants are very important to rainforest animals. Animals use them for food, shade, and protection.

PG 24

Changing Rainforests

Every day parts of rainforests are being cut down by people. When people cut down rainforests, animals lose their homes.

It is important that we take care of rainforests. People need its plants and animals to **survive**.

PG 25

Thousands of trees are cut down every day.

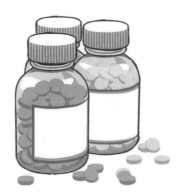

One-forth of all medicines have been discovered in rainforests.

Half of all plants and animals on earth live in rainforests.

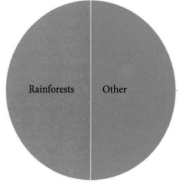

Cacao, the main ingredient in chocolate, was discovered in rainforests.

Glossary

A glossary tells the reader the meaning of important words.

Vines – Thin stems of plants that grow by winding themselves around trees or spreading over the ground

Communicate – To talk to another living animal

Dangerous – Deadly animals, plants, or objects

Poisonous – Something that can cause illness or death

Survive – To stay alive

Draw a picture of the rainforest.

Draw a picture of a rainforest animal.

Quiz

1. Which is the highest layer of rainforests?

a. Canopy

b. Emergent

c. Forest floor

2. Which layer gets the least sunlight?

a. Emergent

b. Forest floor

c. Canopy

3. What does the diagram on page 2 teach you about?

a. The layers of rainforests

b. How trees grow

c. Rainforest animals

Common core standards:
RI. 1. 1 - Questions 1, 2
RI. 1. 6 - Question 3

4. What did the author teach about in the section "Understory"?

a. Animals that live in the forest floor

b. How rain helps the forest grow

c. Animals that live in the understory

5. Which layer is home to the most animals?

a. Canopy

b. Emergent

c. Forest floor

6. Why did the author write the section "Changing Rainforests"?

a. To teach how trees grow in the forest

b. To teach how rainforests are being cut down

c. To explain animal life cycles

Common core standards:

RI. 1. 1 - Questions 5

RI. 1. 2 - Question 4

RI. 1. 8 - Question 6

Want to learn about ocean animals? Check out the "Fay Learns About..." series!

Great for emerging readers ages 6-8

Want to learn about Farm Animals? Check out the "Katie Teaches You About..." series!

Great for early readers ages 4-6

Want to learn about colors? Check out the "Clayton Teaches You About..." series!

Great for early readers ages 4-6

Made in the USA
San Bernardino, CA
25 February 2020

64947826R00024